Little Piggies

Story by Janie Spaht Gill, Ph.D.
Illustrations by Bob Reese

Dominie Press, Inc.

Little piggies don't like going to

SCHOOL.

3

Little piggies like to break
the rules.

5

Little piggies like to stomp,

not walk.

Little piggies like to grunt, not talk.

9

Little piggies sleep

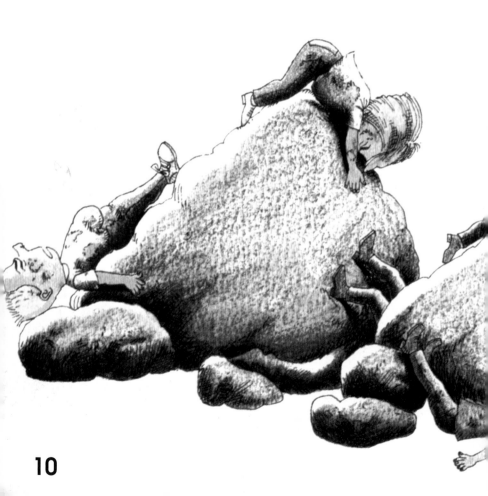

on beds of rock.

Little piggies like old smelly socks.

13

Little piggies wear dirty jeans.

Little piggies wash with greasy things.

Little piggies eat bugs
and weeds.

19

I'm glad I'm not

one of these.

Little Piggies

- Have the children observe each of the "little piggies" in the book and discuss what they could be saying and thinking. Ask the children to name their favorite piggy and explain their choice. Then have them draw or paint their favorite piggy, with a speech bubble over its head. Finally, compile their drawings in a class *Piggy Book*.

- Using a clean, empty, gallon milk jug, make a piggy mask by cutting a hole (the size of a child's head) where the handle of the plastic gallon jug is located. Cut two slits in the top for the ears. The spout acts as the nose. Slip two pink ears through the slits, and glue a pink circle on the spout for the tip of the nose. Glue white construction paper eye sockets with black construction paper pupils pasted inside. The jug sits on top of the child's head like a hat. With their masks on, have the children dramatize the events depicted in the story.

- Have the children write several pages on whether they would like to be themselves or a little piggy. Ask them to explain their choices: "I like being me because I like sleeping in a bed, not on rocks." Then have them illustrate each page. Staple the pages together and make a cover. Now, each child has a *Piggy* book to take home.

About the Author

Dr. Janie Spaht Gill brings twenty-five years of teaching experience to her books for young children. During her career thus far, she has taught at every grade level, from kindergarten through college. Gill has a Ph.D. in reading education, with a minor in creative writing. She is currently residing in Lafayette, Louisiana with her husband, Richard. Her fresh, humorous topics are inspired by the things her students say in the classroom. Gill was voted the 1999-2000 Louisiana Elementary Teacher of the Year for her outstanding work in primary education.

Publisher: Raymond Yuen
Editorial Consultant: Adria F. Klein
Editor: Bob Rowland
Designer: Natalie Chupil
Illustrator: Bob Reese

Published by:

౨ Dominie Press, Inc.

1949 Kellogg Avenue
Carlsbad, California 92008 USA

www.dominie.com
(800) 232-4570

Softcover Edition ISBN 0-7685-2150-5
Library Bound Edition ISBN 0-7685-2458-X

Printed in Singapore by PH Productions Pte Ltd
1 2 3 4 5 6 PH 05 04 03

Dominie Level	Guided Reading	DeFord Assessment
10	F	5